W9-AMW-894

STARTING SCIENCE

WASTE

KAY DAVIES
AND
WENDY OLDFIELD

STECK-VAUGHN
LIBRARY
A Division of Steck-Vaughn Company

Austin, Texas

Starting Science

Books in the series

Animals
Electricity and Magnetism
Floating and Sinking
Food

Light
Sound and Music
Waste
Weather

About This Book

This book takes a look at different types of waste and pollution in situations familiar to children. The children can relate their own experiences to the more general issues surrounding litter, human-made pollution, recycling and cleaning up waste, and nature's way of dealing with waste.

The activities and investigations are designed to be straightforward but fun, and flexible according to the abilities of the children. With the teacher's or parent's guidance they will be introduced to methods in scientific inquiry and recording. The children's involvement in this way should stimulate plenty of discussion.

The main picture and its commentary may be taken as a focal point for further discussion or as an introduction to the topic. Each chapter can form a basis for extended topic work.

Teachers will find that in using this book, they are reinforcing the other core subjects of language and mathematics. By means of its topical approach **Waste** covers many subjects usually taught in the early grades—exploration of science, the variety of life, human influences on the Earth, and types and uses of materials.

©**Copyright this edition 1992**
Steck-Vaughn Company

All rights reserved. No reproduction, copy, or transmission of this publication may be made without permission of the publisher.

Editors: Cally Chambers, Susan Wilson

Typeset by Multifacit Graphics, Keyport, NJ
Printed in Italy by Rotolito Lombarda S.p.A., Milan
Bound in the U.S. by Lake Book, Melrose Park, IL
1 2 3 4 5 6 7 8 9 0 LB 96 95 94 93 92

Library of Congress
Cataloging-in-Publication Data

Davies, Kay.
  Waste / Kay Davies and Wendy Oldfield.
    p.   cm. -- (Starting science)
  Includes bibliographical references (p. 31) and index.
  Summary: Examines various aspects of waste and pollution, including water waste, water pollution, oil spills, litter, air pollution, rust and recycling.
  ISBN 0-8114-3000-6
  1. Refuse and refuse disposal--Juvenile literature.
  2. Pollution--Juvenile literature. 3. Recycling (Waste, etc.)--Juvenile literature. [1. Refuse and refuse disposal. 2. Pollution.] I. Oldfield, Wendy. II. Title. III. Series: Davies, Kay. Starting science.
  TD792.D39 1992   91-23414
  363.72--dc20   CIP AC

CONTENTS

Atlanta-Jackson Twp. Public Library
Atlanta, IN 46031

Words that first appear in **bold** in the text
or captions are explained in the glossary.

92-952

12.96

Steck . Vaughn

6-92

Garbage is moved at the landfill. The seagulls can find scraps to eat there.

A LOAD OF RUBBISH

Where do we put our **trash**? Look for litter baskets and trash cans in the park, at school, and at home.

Ask your teacher if you can look in the trash basket in your classroom. Check it at the end of the day. See what people have thrown away.

Is everything you throw away really trash? Look at these things for instance. What could they be used for?

The plastic cup could be used to store small toys. Rubber bands could keep your pencils together.

WASTEPAPER

Collect things made of paper. Make two piles. One for those things we keep and one for those we throw away.

Our wastepaper can be sent to a factory and made into clean new paper.

You can make your own new paper.

Put scraps of newspaper into a pail with water. Mix it to a **pulp**. Make holes in the lid of a plastic box. Stretch a nylon stocking over the lid. Spread the paper pulp in a thin layer over the lid. Use a rolling pin to flatten the pulp and squeeze the water out. When the pulp is dry, peel it off. Paint a picture on your new paper.

The wood from these trees will be made into paper. Saving paper
will help save trees.

The **compost heap** is piled high with rotting leaves.

GOOD FOR THE GROUND

In the fall, leaves and fruit drop to the ground. These **rot** and become part of the soil. This rot helps new plants to grow.

Rotting fruit becomes soft and brown. Green and white **mold** may grow all over it.

Leave a banana skin and a bruised apple in a plastic bag. Seal the bag.

Draw the changes you see every day. Show how the bruise on your apple grows. Show how the banana skin changes color. Draw in other changes you see.

Day	Apple	Banana skin
1.		
2.		
3.		

Keep your record for a few more days.

Do not touch the moldy fruit. Keep it in the sealed bag.

Everyone is very hungry. They are enjoying their food.

LEFTOVERS

Look at all these scraps and wrappers left in the kitchen.

Sort them into groups like this:

1. Things that will rot and be good for the ground.

2. Things that the birds might like to eat.

3. Things that will be thrown away.

Where can you put your scraps and wrappers?

1. On the compost heap

2. On the bird feeder

3. In the trash can

Remember that even trash can be useful.

The tree stump is dead. But it makes a good home for many types of animals, plants, and **fungi**.

ROTTING WOOD

Wood that lies in damp, dark places begins to change. Small plants and animals, and rain all help to make the wood rot.

Look for a piece of rotting log. Feel it and smell it. How is it different from new wood?

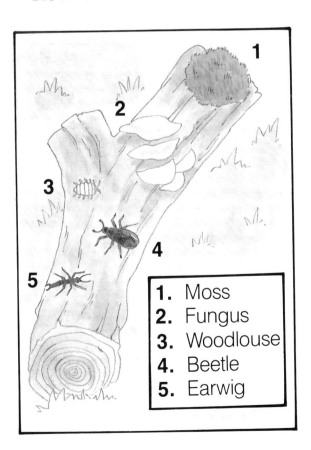

1. Moss
2. Fungus
3. Woodlouse
4. Beetle
5. Earwig

Here are some things that you might find living on your log.

Draw a picture of the log you found. Draw some plants and animals on another piece of paper. Cut them out and paste them on your log picture.

Put the piece of log back where you found it.

WATERWORKS

Every day we use water.

Name all the things you do with water.

Before it reaches us, water must be cleaned. To do this it is passed through layers of **gravel** and sand. These catch the dirt.

Put some water in a pail. Drop garden soil, twigs, leaves, and grass into the water.

Fill a funnel with clean gravel and hold it over an empty pail. Pour some dirty water over the gravel. Can you see any difference in the water?

Do this many times until your water is clean.

The children are giving the dog a bath. The clean water washes the dirt out of its hair.

There are no animals left in this pond. Trash has made the pond's water dirty.

DEAD WATER

Most animals cannot live in dirty water.

Try this in the summer. Put some dirty dishwater in one pail and some fresh, clean water from a pond or stream into another.

Leave them outside. Use a jar to take **samples**. Look at a new sample every week. You will need a magnifying glass.

The dirty water begins to smell. Not many animals can live in this water.

The clean water is full of tiny living things.

Fish and birds eat tiny living things. So a clean pond can make a good home for fish and birds.

OIL CAN SPOIL

Find two dry, fluffy feathers. Throw them in the air. Watch them float gently to the ground.

Dip one feather in some cooking oil. The feather looks sticky and heavy.

Throw the feathers in the air again. What do you notice now?

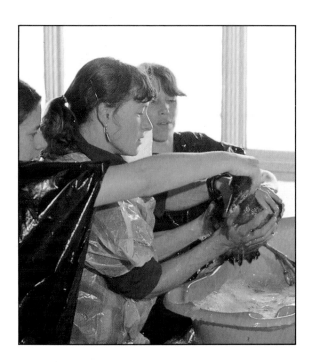

Most birds with oil on their feathers cannot fly.

People sometimes rescue birds that have been covered in oil.

They try to clean the sticky oil from their feathers with soapy water.

Oil from a shipwreck spills into the ocean. It can kill seabirds when it sticks to their feathers.

WHAT A MESS!

Look for **litter** on your way to school. Look in the park. Look in the shopping center. Notice where the dirtiest place is.

Do you think it is nice to see litter? Where would you put it?

Litter makes our towns and countryside messy. It can also be dangerous.

Make a "Don't Litter" poster. Paint a big litter basket. Paste things you do not want on the basket.

Think of other ways to keep people from littering.

You could start a "Clean Up Litter" project in your school.

Everybody has had fun at the seashore. But look at all the litter they have left behind.

Factories and cars give out smoke, soot, and fumes. This **pollution** makes the air we breathe dirty. It can make us feel ill.

CLOUD OF SMOKE

How dirty is your air?

Put some light-colored jelly in a pitcher. Carefully pour in some hot water to make it runny. Fill some shallow bowls with the jelly and water.

Leave your bowls in different places outside. Try a windowsill, a sidewalk, and a place near a door.

Look at your bowls after two days.

You can see how much dirt and dust has collected on the jelly.

The dirtiest bowl shows where there was the most air pollution.

23

These old pieces of metal are covered with **rust**. The rust has eaten away the shiny metal.

OLD IRON

Half fill a jar with water. Put a clean, shiny, iron nail in the water.

Look closely at your jar every day.

Soon you will notice that the nail begins to rust. The water turns brown, too.

Try other metal things to see if they rust. Try things like bottle caps, screws and bolts, paper clips, hairpins, and safety pins. Use a different jar for each object.

Look for changes every day.

Only the things made of iron will rust.

SOMEBODY'S HOME

Some birds build their nests with dried grass, moss, and twigs.

Sometimes they use pieces of string and plastic which we have thrown away.

Can you make a nest?

An old pot makes a home for this bird and her babies.

Can you make a home out of trash? You could use cardboard boxes, sticks, old blankets, leaves, and string.

The blackbird has made a nest for her babies. Can you see the bits of plastic she has used?

The model has been put together from all sorts of trash
by an artist. Can you recognize the things that have been
used to make it?

SOMETHING FROM NOTHING

You can make a model from throw-away things.

Try to make a caterpillar train like this.

1. Cut apart an egg carton.

2. Bend the end over and paste it down to make the head.

3. Make two small holes in the head. Use toothpicks with clay on the ends for the eyes.

4. Paint your caterpillar train.

Use the caterpillar to hold coins, paper clips, or other small things.

Make some more models from other kinds of boxes and cartons.

GLOSSARY

Compost heap A mixture of leaves and other things that will rot.

Factory A place where machines are used to make things.

Fungus (plural: **Fungi**) A living growth found in damp places. It is not an animal or a plant.

Gravel A mixture of small stones.

Litter Small pieces of rubbish, sometimes carelessly thrown away.

Mold A furry fungus that grows on rotting food.

Pollution Anything that spoils the soil, water, or air.

Pulp Usually paper or wood that has been made wet and soft.

Rot When changes take place in living things, making them soft and causing them to waste away.

Rust A red-brown covering on iron that has been wet or damp.

Samples Small amounts of something, showing what the rest is like.

Trash Things, such as paper, scraps of food, and bottles and cans, that are thrown away.

PICTURE ACKNOWLEDGMENTS

Bruce Coleman Ltd. 4 (Price), 12 (Krasemann); Chapel Studios (Zul Mukhida) 5, 6, 9, 13, 14, 18 top, 20, 21, 23 both, 25 both, 26 top, 29; Eye Ubiquitous 11 (Seheult), 28 (Parkin); Eric and David Hosking 7; Frank Lane Picture Agency 26 bottom (Withers), 27 (Wilmshurst); ©James Minor cover; Oxford Scientific Films 16 (Chillmaid); Papilio 8, 24; Photri 19; Rex Features 18 bottom; Tim Woodcock 10; ZEFA 15, 22.

Artwork illustrations by Rebecca Archer.

FINDING OUT MORE

Books to read:

50 Simple Things Kids Can Do to Recycle (Earthworks, 1991)
How Green Are You? by David Bellamy (Clarkson Potter, 1991)

The following groups will be able to help you find out more about waste and pollution.

Acid Rain Foundation
1410 Varsity Dr.
Raleigh, NC 27606

Conservation Foundation
1250 24th St. NW
Washington, DC 20037

Friends of the Earth
530 Seventh St. SE
Washington, DC 20003

Greenpeace USA
1436 U St. NW
Washington, DC 20009

Sierra Club
730 Polk St.
San Francisco, CA 94109

INDEX

First published in 1990 by Wayland
(Publishers) Ltd.
©Copyright 1990 Wayland (Publishers) Ltd.